For more than forty years,
Yearling has been the leading name
in classic and award-winning literature
for young readers.

Yearling books feature children's
favorite authors and characters,
providing dynamic stories of adventure,
humor, history, mystery, and fantasy.

Trust Yearling paperbacks to entertain,
inspire, and promote the love of reading
in all children.

HOW BIG IS A
FOOT?

OTHER YEARLING BOOKS YOU WILL ENJOY

THE BEAST IN MS. ROONEY'S ROOM, *Patricia Reilly Giff*

SNAGGLE DOODLES, *Patricia Reilly Giff*

OLIVIA SHARP: THE PRINCESS OF THE
FILLMORE STREET SCHOOL
Marjorie Weinman Sharmat and Mitchell Sharmat

FRECKLE JUICE, *Judy Blume*

THE ONE IN THE MIDDLE IS THE GREEN KANGAROO
Judy Blume

THE STORIES JULIAN TELLS, *Ann Cameron*

GLORIA RISING, *Ann Cameron*

*WRITTEN
AND ILLUSTRATED BY*
ROLF MYLLER

HOW BIG IS A

FOOT?

A YEARLING BOOK

Visit us on the Web! www.randomhouse.com/kids

Educators and librarians, for a variety of teaching tools, visit us at
www.randomhouse.com/teachers

ISBN: 0-440-40495-9

Reprinted by arrangement with the author

Printed in the United States of America

August 1991

40

OPM

*To the wonderful metric system
without whose absence in this country
this book would not have been possible*

HOW BIG IS A
FOOT?

Once upon a time
there lived a King
and his wife, the Queen.

They were a happy couple
for they had everything in the World.

However . . .

when the Queen's birthday came near

the King had a problem:

What could he give to Someone

who had Everything?

The King thought

and he thought and he thought.

Until suddenly, he had an idea!

HE WOULD GIVE THE QUEEN A BED.

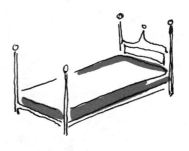

The Queen did not have a bed

because at the time

beds had not been invented.

So even Someone who had Everything—

did not have a bed.

The King called his Prime Minister

and asked him to please have a bed made.

The Prime Minister called the Chief Carpenter

and asked him to please have a bed made.

The Chief Carpenter called the apprentice

and told him to make a bed.

"How big is a bed?" asked the apprentice,

who didn't know because at the time

nobody had ever seen a bed.

"How big is a bed?"

the Carpenter asked the Prime Minister.

"A good question," said the Prime Minister.

And he asked the King,

"HOW BIG *IS* A BED?"

The King thought and

he thought and he thought.

Until suddenly he had an idea!

THE BED

MUST BE BIG ENOUGH TO FIT THE QUEEN.

The King called the Queen.

He told her to put on her new pajamas

and told her to lie on the floor.

The King took off his shoes

and with his big feet

walked carefully around the Queen.

He counted that

the bed must be

THREE FEET WIDE AND SIX FEET LONG

to be big enough to fit the Queen.

(Including the crown

which the Queen sometimes liked to wear to sleep.)

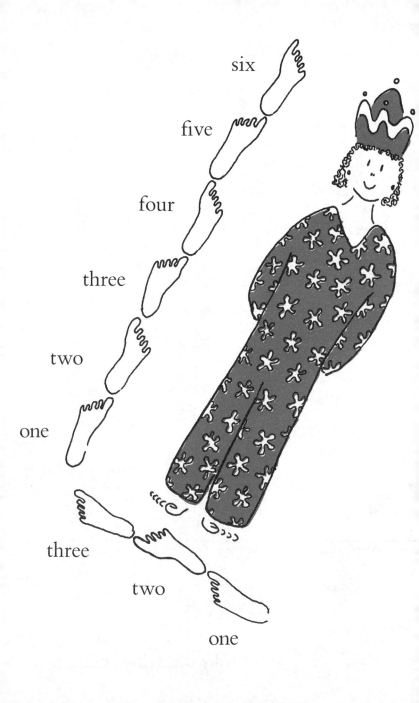

six

five

four

three

two

one

three

two

one

The King said "Thank you," to the Queen,

and told the Prime Minister,

who told the Chief Carpenter,

who told the apprentice:

"The bed must be

three feet wide and six feet long

to be big enough to fit the Queen."

(Including the crown

which she sometimes liked to wear to sleep.)

The apprentice said "Thank you,"

and took off his shoes,

and with his little feet

he measured

six feet long

and

three feet wide

and made a bed to fit the Queen.

When the King saw the bed,

he thought it was beautiful.

He could not wait for the Queen's Birthday.

Instead, he called the Queen at once
and told her to put on her new pajamas.

Then he brought out the bed
and told the Queen to try it.

BUT

the bed was much too small for the Queen.

The King was so angry that he immediately

       called the Prime Minister

       who called the Chief Carpenter

       who called the jailer

who threw the apprentice into jail.

The apprentice was unhappy.

WHY WAS THE BED
TOO SMALL FOR THE QUEEN?

He thought and

    he thought and he thought.

    Until suddenly he had an idea!

A bed that was three King's feet wide
and six King's feet long
was naturally bigger than
a bed that was three apprentice feet wide
and six apprentice feet long.

"I CAN MAKE A BED
TO FIT THE QUEEN
IF I KNOW THE SIZE
OF THE KING'S FOOT,"

he cried.

He explained this to the jailer,

who explained it to the Chief Carpenter,

who explained it to the Prime Minister,

who explained it to the King,

who was much too busy to go to the jail.

Instead, the King took off one shoe

and called a famous sculptor.

The sculptor made an exact marble copy

of the King's foot.

This was sent to the jail.

The apprentice took the marble copy
of the King's foot,

and with it he measured

three feet wide

and six feet long

and built a bed to fit the Queen!

The Bed was ready just in time
for the Queen's Birthday.

The King called the Queen
and told her to put on her new pajamas.

Then he brought out the New Bed
and told the Queen to try it.

The Queen got into bed and . . .

THE BED FIT THE QUEEN PERFECTLY.

(Including the crown

    which she sometimes liked

        to wear to sleep.)

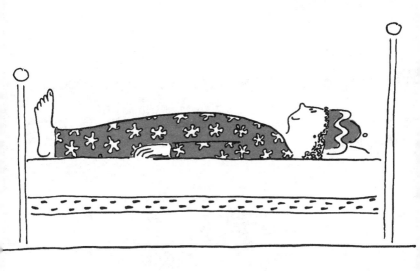

It was, without a doubt, the nicest gift that the Queen had ever received.

The King was very happy.

He immediately called the apprentice

from jail and made him a royal prince.

He ordered a big parade, and all the people

came out to cheer the little apprentice prince.

And forever after,

anyone who wanted to measure

anything

used a copy of the King's foot.

And when someone said,

"My bed is six feet long

and three feet wide,"

everyone knew exactly how big it was.